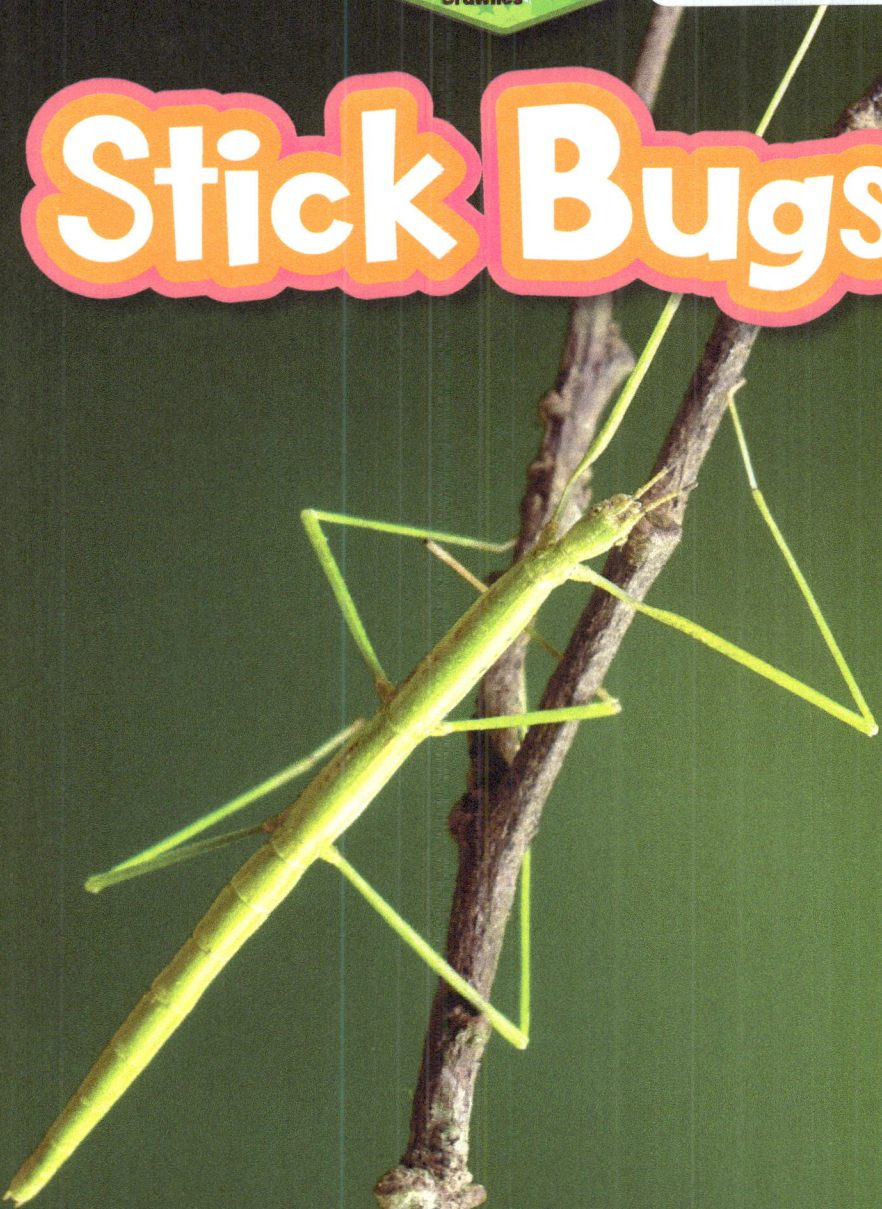

Backyard Bugs & Creepy-Crawlies

Stick Bugs

Ashley Lee

Explore other books at:
WWW.ENGAGEBOOKS.COM

VANCOUVER, B.C.

e → WWW.ENGAGEBOOKS.COM

Stick Bugs: Level 1
Backyard Bugs & Creepy Crawlies
Lee, Ashley 1995 –
Text © 2022 Engage Books
Design © 2022 Engage Books

Edited by: A.R. Roumanis

Text set in Epilogue

FIRST EDITION / FIRST PRINTING

LIBRARY AND ARCHIVES CANADA CATALOGUING IN PUBLICATION

Title: Stick Bugs / Ashley Lee.
Names: Lee, Ashley, author.
Description: Series statement: Backyard bugs & creepy-crawlies
Engaging readers: level 1, beginner.

Identifiers: Canadiana (print) 20250448542 | Canadiana (ebook) 20250448569
ISBN 978-1-77878-711-9 (hardcover)
ISBN 978-1-77878-720-1 (softcover)

Subjects:
LCSH: Stick Bugs—Juvenile literature.

Classification: LCC QL737.P94 C38 2025 | DDC J599.885—DC23

This project has been made possible in part by the Government of Canada.

Canadä

Contents

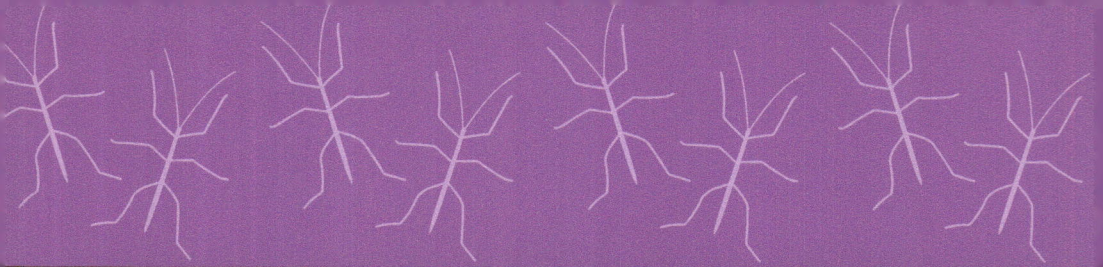

What Are Stick Bugs?

Stick bugs are insects that are really good at hiding. They look just like sticks!

There are many different kinds of stick bugs. The larger kinds are some of the longest insects on Earth.

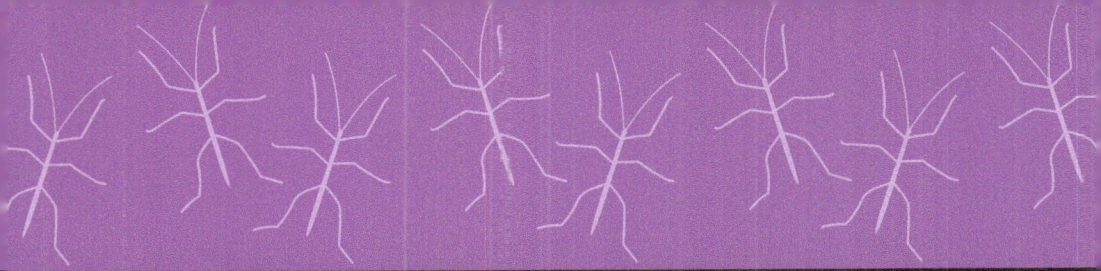

5

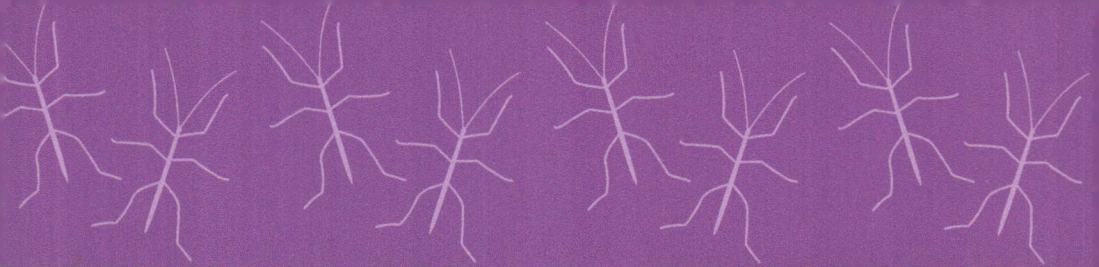

What Do Stick Bugs Look Like?

Stick bugs are often brown, green, or gray. They often have long bodies.

Stick bugs have long feelers. They help stick bugs feel what is around them.

Feelers

Stick bugs often have long, thin legs. They can **detach** them and grow new ones.

8

Some stick bugs have wings. Most are not very good at flying.

Where Do Stick Bugs Live?

Stick bugs live everywhere except Antarctica. The largest stick bugs live in **tropical** areas.

Key Word

Tropical: areas that are hot with lots of rain year-round.

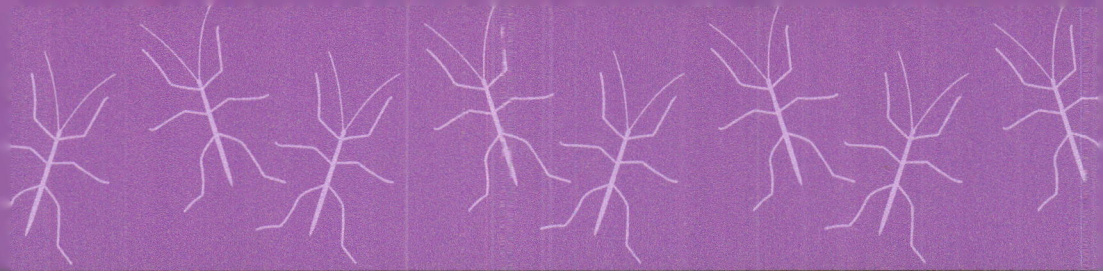

Stick bugs often live in forests. This makes it easy for them to blend in.

What Do Stick Bugs Eat?

Stick bugs are herbivores. Herbivores are animals that only eat plants.

Stick bugs mostly eat leaves. They like some leaves more than others.

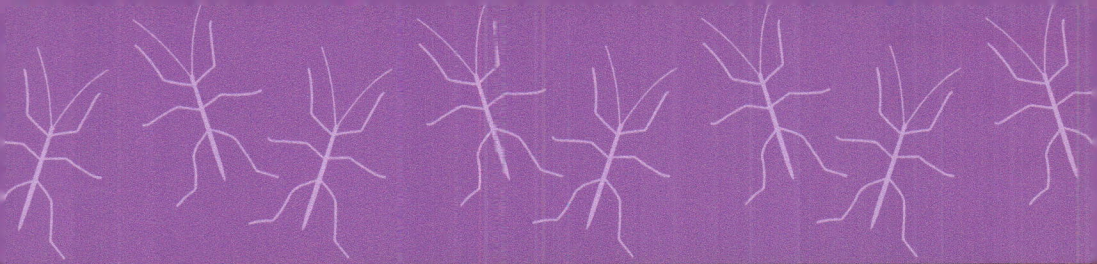

Stick Bug Behavior

Stick bugs are mostly active at night. This helps them stay away from daytime **predators**.

Key Word

Predators: animals that hunt and eat other animals.

14

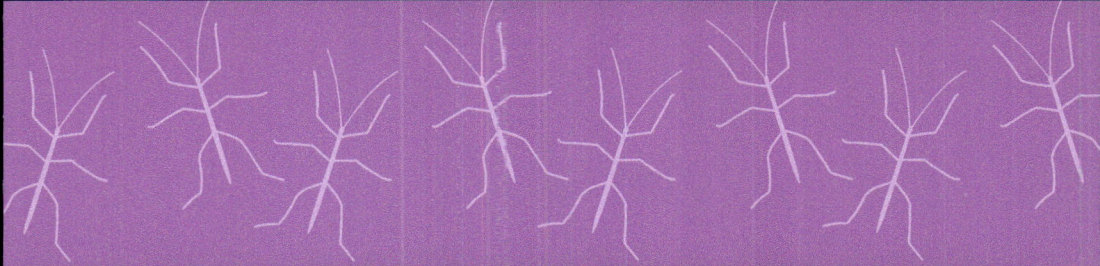

Stick bugs sway when they walk to make it look like they are just a branch in the wind.

15

Different stick bugs have different ways of **defending** themselves against other animals.

Key Word

Defending: protecting from harm.

16

Some stick bugs have spikes on their legs. Others can make a spray that blinds other animals.

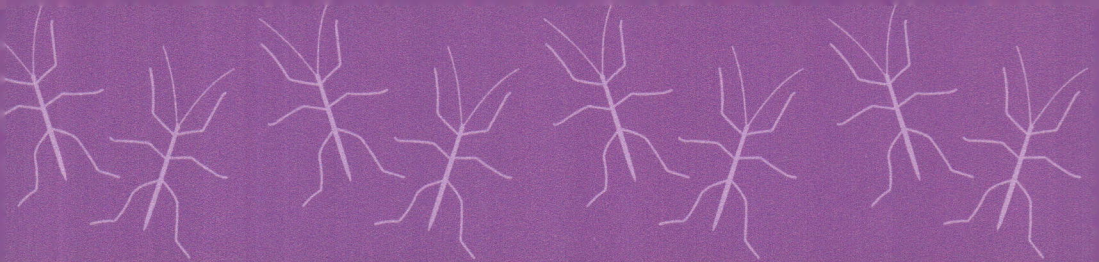

Stick Bug Life Cycle

Some stick bugs drop their eggs on the ground. Others lay eggs in places that are hard to get to or see.

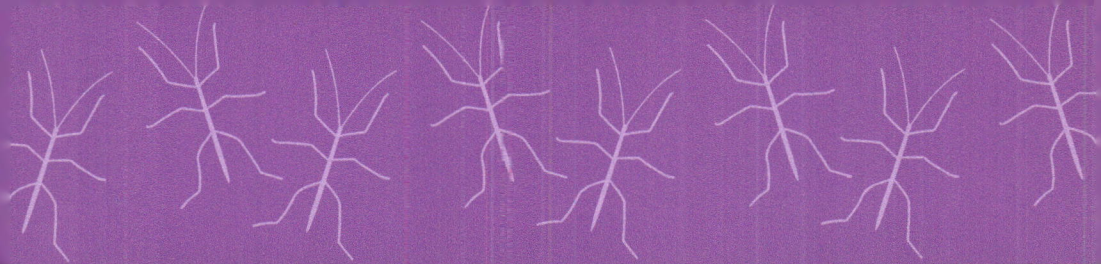

Stick bug eggs often look like seeds. They take two months to one year to hatch.

Baby stick bugs
are called nymphs.
Nymphs shed their
skin. This helps
them grow.

Stick bugs have short lives. They live for six to eight months.

Fun Facts

The longest stick bug ever found was as long as two pieces of paper!

A female stick bug can make babies all by herself.

Many stick
bugs eat the
skin they shed.

Stick bugs
often hang
upside down
when shedding
their skin.

23

Stick bugs breathe through holes in their bodies called spiracles.

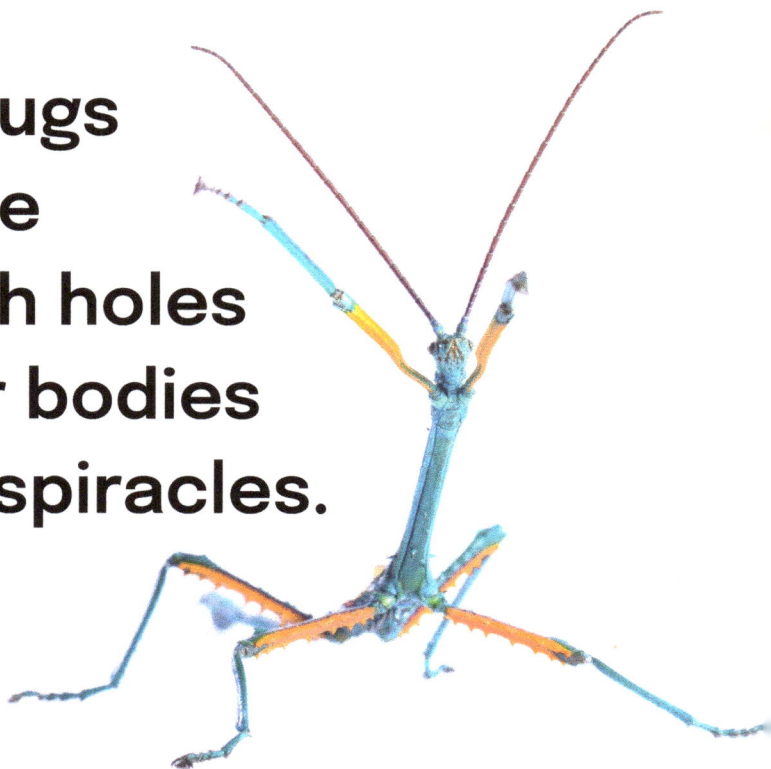

Stick bugs are also called ghost insects.

Ants sometimes take stick bug eggs home with them. The eggs hatch safely in ant hills.

Stick bugs are sometimes kept as pets.

Are Stick Bugs Helpful or Harmful?

Stick bugs are helpful! Eating leaves off of plants helps new ones grow.

Stick bugs are also
food for many animals.
There would be
less food
without them.

Are Stick Bugs in Danger?

Most stick bugs are in danger. They are dying out.

People are taking over the places they live. They destroy them to make buildings or farms.

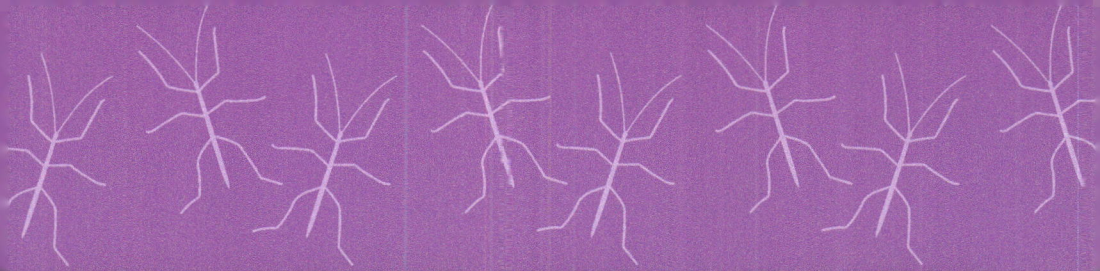

29

Quiz

Test your knowledge of stick bugs by answering the following questions. The questions are based on what you have read in this book. The answers are listed on the bottom of the next page.

1 Are stick bugs insects?

2 Are most stick bugs good at flying?

3 Do stick bugs often live in forests?

4 Do some stick bugs have spikes on their legs?

5 Can a female stick bug make babies all by herself?

6 Are stick bugs food for many animals?

Explore other books in the
Backyard Bugs & Creepy Crawlies series!

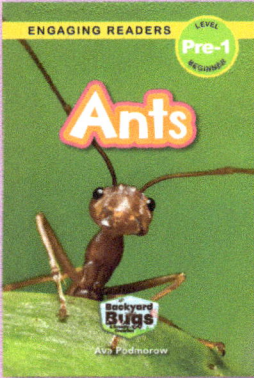

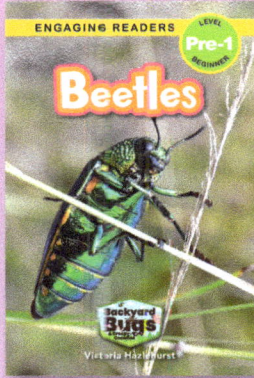

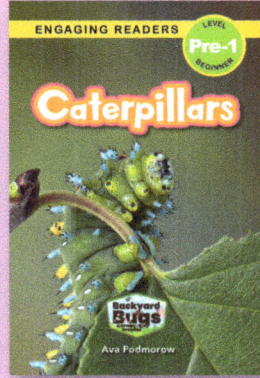

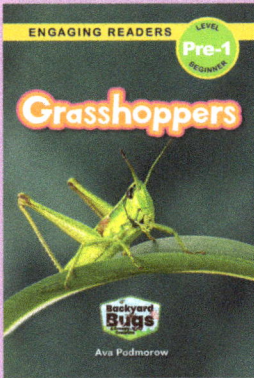

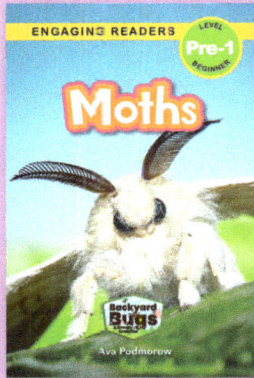

Visit www.engagebooks.com to explore more Engaging Readers.

www.ingramcontent.com/pod-product-compliance
Lightning Source LLC
Chambersburg PA
CBHW052037030426
42337CB00027B/5037